WE THE PEOPLE

September 11

by Mary Englar

Content Advisers: John Mulligan, Assistant Fire Commissioner, Ret.,
Fire Department of the City of New York
Barbara Elias, 9/11 Policy Analyst, The National Security Archive,
George Washington University

Reading Adviser: Rosemary G. Palmer, Ph.D., Department of Literacy,
College of Education, Boise State University

COMPASS POINT BOOKS
MINNEAPOLIS, MINNESOTA

Compass Point Books
3109 West 50th Street, #115
Minneapolis, MN 55410

Visit Compass Point Books on the Internet at *www.compasspointbooks.com*
or e-mail your request to *custserv@compasspointbooks.com*

On the cover: Firefighters raise a flag at the site of the World Trade Center.

Photographs ©: Getty Images/Thomas E. Franklin/The Bergen Record, cover; Prints Old and Rare,
back cover (far left); Library of Congress, back cover; Corbis/Reuters, 5, 11, 12, 14, 16, 19, 20, 21,
30, 36, 37, 41; Corbis/Sean Adair/Reuters, 7; FDNY Photo Unit, 9, 32; Getty Images/Joe Raedle, 13;
Getty Images/Photo by Mario Tama, 17; Photodisc, 23; Corbis/Martin H. Simon, 24; Todd M. Beamer
Foundation, 26; Getty Images/David Maxwell/AFP, 27; Getty Images/Andrea Booher/FEMA, 28; Getty
Images/Doug Kanter/AFP, 29, 38, 39; Getty Images/U.S. Navy Photo by David C. Mercil, 34; Getty
Images/Johnny Bivera, 35.

Editor: Sue Vander Hook
Page Production: Blue Tricycle
Photo Researchers: Abbey Fitzgerald and Marcie C. Spence
Cartographer: XNR Productions, Inc.
Library Consultant: Kathleen Baxter

Creative Director: Keith Griffin
Editorial Director: Carol Jones
Managing Editor: Catherine Neitge

Library of Congress Cataloging-in-Publication Data
Englar, Mary
  September 11 / by Mary Englar
    p. cm.—(We the people)
Includes bibliographical references and index.
  ISBN-13: 978-0-7565-2029-8 (hardcover)
  ISBN-10: 0-7565-2029-0 (hardcover)
  ISBN-13: 978-0-7565-2041-0 (paperback)
  ISBN-10: 0-7565-2041-X (paperback)
1. September 11 Terrorist Attacks, 2001—Juvenile literature. 2. Terrorism—United States—Juvenile
literature. 3. War on Terrorism, 2001—Juvenile literature. I. Title. II. We the people (Series) (Compass
Point Books)
  HV6432.7.E52 2007
  973.931—dc22   2006003941

TABLE OF CONTENTS

SURPRISE ATTACK

Tuesday, September 11, 2001, was warm and clear in New York City. People were arriving on trains, subways, buses, and cars on their way to work. Others walked, enjoying the morning sun. At about 8:45 A.M., Barry Meier was walking down Greenwich Street when he heard a loud roar. He looked up and saw "a huge silver jet ... flying closer to the ground than I had ever seen."

Across the East River in Brooklyn, Chief Peter J. Ganci Jr., the head of the Fire Department of the City of New York (FDNY), looked out the window at 8:46 A.M. and also saw the jet. He jumped to his feet and shouted to Chief of Operations Daniel Nigro. A huge plane had just hit the North Tower of the World Trade Center.

They stared out the window as a fireball burst from the 110-story building. Ganci and other fire chiefs rushed to their cars and raced over the Brooklyn Bridge

People in Times Square watched the North Tower burn on September 11, 2001.

toward the disaster.

People in the streets below bent their heads back to see what had happened. Fire and thick black smoke

5

spewed from a gaping hole between the 93rd and 99th floors. Pieces of steel, airplane parts, debris, and clouds of office papers fell from the huge opening.

Inside the North Tower, people felt a thud as the plane crashed into the building. They didn't know what had happened. Some thought it was an earthquake. Workers on floors below the crash site saw black smoke billowing past their windows. They hurried to evacuate as smoke filled the stairwells, offices, and elevators.

Seventeen minutes later, at 9:03 A.M., another tragedy struck. A second airplane crashed into the other World Trade Center tower. Most of the 16,000 to 18,000 people in the two towers didn't know that planes had collided into their buildings. As smoke filled their offices, they only knew they had to try to get out.

At 9:25 A.M., the Federal Aviation Administration ordered all airplanes over the United States to land immediately. But by 9:37 A.M., a third airplane smashed into the Pentagon building, headquarters of the U.S.

As the North Tower burned, a second plane crashed into the South Tower and exploded.

7

Department of Defense near Washington, D.C.

Twenty-six minutes later, at 10:03 A.M., a fourth hijacked plane crashed near Shanksville, Pennsylvania, about 150 miles (240 kilometers) from Washington, D.C. The world watched as television cameras focused on burning buildings that once stood as symbols of American strength.

Four American airplanes were hijacked and intentionally crashed that day. All 256 people onboard those planes died. Another 2,595 people died at the World Trade Center, which became known as Ground Zero. Among the dead were 343 New York City firefighters and 60 police officers. The crash at the Pentagon killed another 125 people.

The September 11 attack was the deadliest in U.S. history. At first, no one knew who was responsible. But people inside the U.S. government who studied terrorism began to accuse a terrorist group known as al-Qaeda, which means "the base" in the Arabic language.

A skeletonlike shell was all that remained after the Twin Towers collapsed.

Al-Qaeda and its leader, Osama bin Laden, would soon be well-known to Americans and people all over the world.

THE DEADLY PLAN

Everyone wanted to know who had done this and why. Nineteen hijackers had carried out the deadly plan. They were from Saudi Arabia, Egypt, Lebanon, and the United Arab Emirates. On September 11, 2001, they boarded four airplanes. Some got on in Boston, Massachusetts; some in Newark, New Jersey; and others at Dulles International Airport near Washington, D.C. All the planes were scheduled to take off at about 8 A.M. Each man carried a one-way ticket to Los Angeles or San Francisco.

The hijackers belonged to al-Qaeda, a group founded in 1988 by bin Laden to train Muslims, people who belong to the religion of Islam, to fight against people he called the enemies of Islam. Bin Laden believed U.S. foreign policies and American society were harming Muslims in the Middle East and destroying Muslim culture.

Members of al-Qaeda were encouraged to wage war against any government that they thought was harming

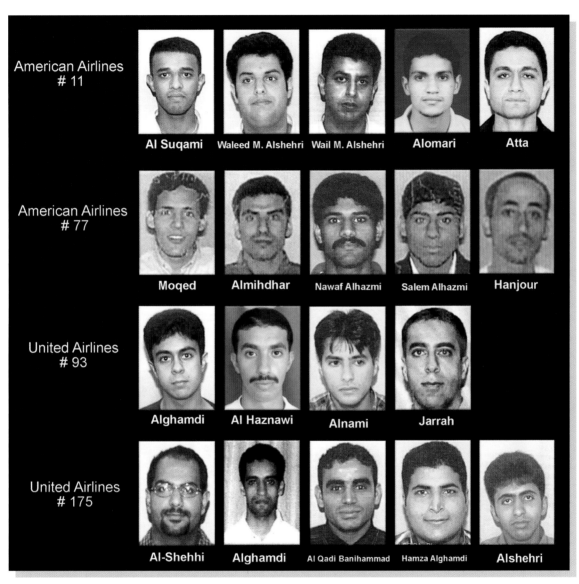

On September 27, 2001, the U.S. Department of Justice released pictures of the 19 suspected hijackers.

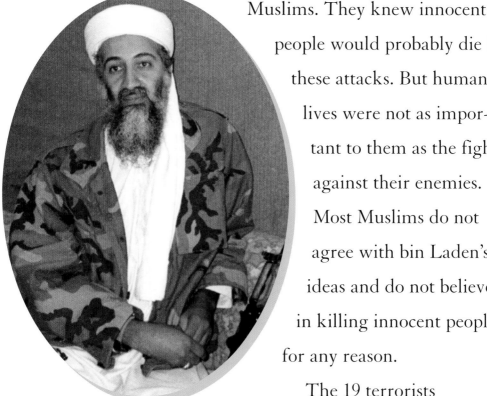

Osama bin Laden,
leader of al-Qaeda

Muslims. They knew innocent people would probably die in these attacks. But human lives were not as important to them as the fight against their enemies. Most Muslims do not agree with bin Laden's ideas and do not believe in killing innocent people for any reason.

The 19 terrorists who boarded airplanes on September 11 were followers of bin Laden. Only a few leaders of al-Qaeda knew about the plan to hijack commercial airplanes and use them as weapons against the United States.

The plan took several years to develop. During those years, at least four terrorists learned to fly U.S. Boeing jets

Terrorist Ziad Samir Jarrah and two other terrorists are believed to have taken flying lessons at the Florida Flight Training Center at the Venice Municipal Airport.

at American flight schools. They planned to crash their hijacked planes at the same time so the United States could not fight back. They chose planes that carried thousands of gallons of jet fuel. They knew the fuel would catch fire and explode like a bomb, creating more destruction.

13

TWO PLANES AND THE WORLD TRADE CENTER

At about 7:30 A.M. on September 11, five terrorists boarded American Airlines Flight 11 at Logan International Airport in Boston, Massachusetts. At 8:15 A.M., they broke into the cockpit and took over the controls. Thirty-one

A surveillance video showed two hijackers passing through airport security on the morning of September 11, 2001.

minutes later, at 8:46 A.M., the airplane smashed into the North Tower of the World Trade Center in New York City.

Most people thought this was a terrible accident, not an attack. When it struck, a fireball blew out windows on all four sides of the building. People in the neighboring South Tower felt their building sway from the force of the crash. Fortunately, the plane struck before 9 A.M., and many people had not yet arrived at work.

About 10,000 gallons (38,000 liters) of exploding jet fuel gushed down elevator shafts and spewed out the building. Some people on the street below were burned or struck by pieces of metal from the building and the plane. Many ran away from the towers. Others were so frightened that they stood for many minutes looking up at the burning tower.

Inside the building, fire and smoke spread quickly. Thousands of people fled down emergency stairways. It took some people more than an hour to walk from the 90th floor to the lobby. John Labriola worked on the 71st floor. He remembered that everyone stayed calm and tried

Many workers evacuated both towers after the first airplane crashed into the North Tower.

to help each other. One man carried a woman down the steps because she couldn't make it on her own.

One minute after the first plane crashed, the FDNY and the New York Police Department (NYPD) received the first alarm. More than 1,000 first responders rushed to the World Trade Center.

Emergency treatment centers were set up nearby.

Workers in the South Tower watched as thick smoke streamed from the North Tower. They began to evacuate. This early evacuation saved many lives. Seventeen minutes after the first plane hit, at 9:03 A.M., United Airlines Flight

People fled the area of the World Trade Center after two airplanes hit the buildings.

175 crashed into the South Tower between the 77th and 85th floors. Most people inside didn't know what was happening. Some used cell phones to call family members, who told them that planes had hit both towers.

While people evacuated, the FDNY and the NYPD set up command centers in both tower lobbies. Chief Ganci sent firefighters into the North Tower. Hundreds of firefighters climbed the emergency stairs to rescue people and direct them to safety. During the first hour after the attacks, thousands of people escaped from both buildings.

17

The Twin Towers, as they were called, were designed in the 1960s to withstand a plane crash. But airplanes got larger and carried more fuel since the towers were designed. Some people warned that the towers might collapse. At 9:59 A.M., people on the street heard a loud roaring sound. They looked up and saw the South Tower collapsing. As people ran to get away, each floor crashed onto the floor below, forcing the entire tower to collapse. More than 100,000 tons (90,000 metric tons) of steel and concrete tumbled to the ground in less than one minute. It happened so quickly that many firefighters, police officers, and workers still in the building didn't have time to get out.

A huge cloud of crushed debris, dust, ash, and smoke filled city streets for many blocks. Everyone tried to run away, but some were injured or killed by pieces of the tower. Survivors covered with dirt and ashes struggled to breathe.

Ganci and 75 firefighters were at the command post near the North Tower when the South Tower collapsed. Firefighter Steve Mosiello told how they escaped into an

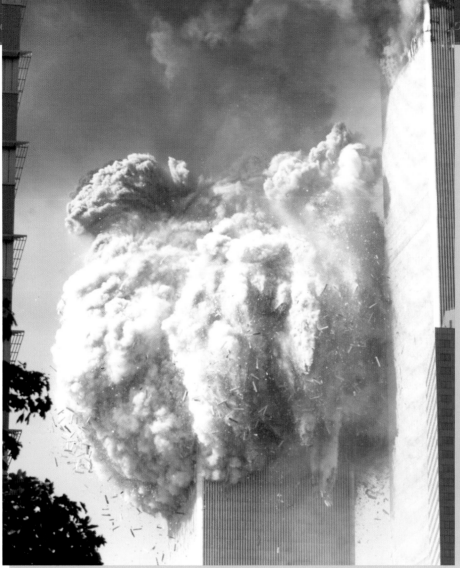

The South Tower after it began to collapse

underground garage. "There was dust everywhere. Every-one had trouble breathing," he recalled. Ganci and two other firefighters headed into the North Tower to help firefighters still in the building. Then they were ordered to get out

The North Tower tumbled into a heap 29 minutes after the South Tower fell.

immediately. Some heard the order, but many did not.

At 10:28 A.M., the North Tower collapsed. Ganci and hundreds of others were killed. People on the street heard the thunderous noise and ran. Many looked back in disbelief that both towers had now fallen. It was hard to understand how anyone could have done this on purpose.

For more than 30 years, the Twin Towers had stood majestically above New York City. Along with the Empire State Building, the towers had defined the Lower Manhattan skyline for as long as many could remember. Now, in only 102 minutes, these huge skyscrapers lay in a seven-story pile of twisted metal and burning rubble.

THE PENTAGON AND FLIGHT 93

While firefighters were scrambling to help people at the World Trade Center, American Airlines Flight 77 was flying toward the nation's capital. Around 9:30 A.M., an air traffic controller at Dulles International Airport near Washington, D.C., saw an unknown plane flying low and fast toward the U.S. capital.

The airport contacted officials at the White House at 9:33 A.M. to warn the president of a possible threat. President George W. Bush was in Sarasota, Florida, speaking to second-graders. But Vice President Dick Cheney, first lady Laura Bush, and others were at the White House. They were quickly rushed to safe places.

Inside the Pentagon, many workers were watching television coverage of the events in New York City. Although they worked at the headquarters of the U.S. Department of Defense, none of them knew a plane was headed toward their building. At 9:37 A.M., a commercial airplane swooped low enough to clip streetlights on a nearby road and then crashed directly into the side of the Pentagon. The crash killed everyone on the plane and 125 workers inside the building. More than 100 people were

The Pentagon, near Washington, D.C., is headquarters for the U.S. Department of Defense.

rushed to area hospitals with serious injuries.

Meanwhile, United Airlines Flight 93, the last of the hijacked airplanes, took off later than scheduled. At 8:42 A.M., it left Newark, New Jersey, heading to San Francisco. But by 9:30 A.M., it had changed its westerly course and was flying east over Ohio.

Cleveland Air Traffic Control received a radio call of "Mayday," an international distress signal for "Help!" There were sounds of a struggle and a voice saying, "Hey,

The attack on the Pentagon forced thousands of workers to evacuate.

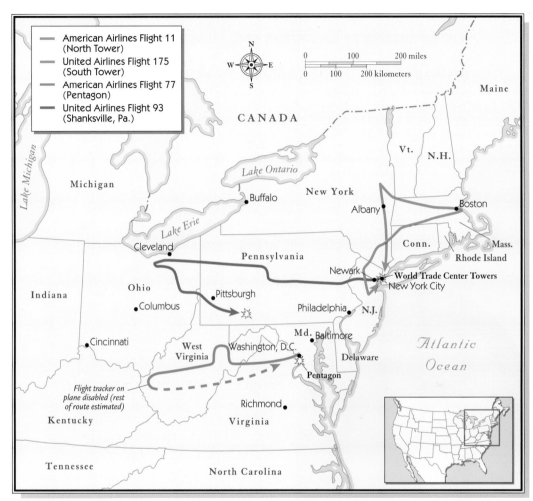

Legend:
- American Airlines Flight 11 (North Tower)
- United Airlines Flight 175 (South Tower)
- American Airlines Flight 77 (Pentagon)
- United Airlines Flight 93 (Shanksville, Pa.)

Flight paths of the four hijacked airplanes on September 11, 2001

get out of here!" The call came from the cockpit of Flight
93. Flight attendants called airline headquarters and said
four hijackers had stabbed a passenger, broken into the
cockpit, and taken control of the airplane.

25

The hijackers had knives and forced passengers to the back of the plane where some used phones to call family members. These passengers heard about the World Trade center and feared their plane might also be used by terrorists to destroy an important building.

Flight attendant Sandy Bradshaw called her husband and said she was going to throw hot water on the terrorists.

Passenger Todd Beamer talked to a telephone operator for about 15 minutes. He told her that some of the passengers were going to jump the hijackers. The last words she heard him say were, "Are you guys ready? Let's roll."

The cockpit voice recorder picked up sounds of a desperate struggle outside the cockpit door. Some passengers were trying to break in. The

Todd Beamer (1968–2001), passenger on United Airlines Flight 93

26

On September 12, 2001, investigators inspected the Flight 93 crash site in Pennsylvania.

terrorist pilot rocked the plane back and forth to throw the passengers off their feet. But the passengers didn't give up.

Several minutes later, at 10:03 A.M., Flight 93 crashed into an empty field near Shanksville, Pennsylvania. All onboard were killed. The actions of those brave passengers probably prevented the terrorists from crashing into the White House or the Capitol Building in Washington, D.C.

"THE BEST OF AMERICA"

Rescue workers from all over the country headed to New York City and Washington, D.C. Firefighters, police officers, construction workers, and medics offered to search for survivors and care for the injured. More than 300 trained dogs came to search for people still trapped in the

Mike Scott from California Task Force-8 and his dog, Billy, searched the rubble for victims.

A man standing at Ground Zero called out asking if anyone needed help.

rubble. Some of the dogs wore cameras to help rescuers look for survivors.

At the World Trade Center site, only 18 people were pulled alive from the rubble. Twelve others were rescued from a stairwell that protected them during the collapse.

29

Posters of the missing hung on bus shelters, railroad stations, fences, walls, and lampposts.

Thousands of people were missing. Relatives searched every hospital, hoping to find their husbands, wives, sisters, brothers, or parents. They posted pictures of their loved ones on almost every lamppost and store window. Dust-covered photographs labeled with the word *Missing*

30

blanketed the city. Residents of New York, one of the most lively cities in the world, were shocked and heartbroken. They had lost more than 2,000 people in a matter of minutes.

After 48 hours, no more survivors were found. Meanwhile, the U.S. military watched for more possible attacks. Fighter jets patrolled the skies over the country's major cities. Helicopters circled Washington, D.C., and U.S. warships guarded the East Coast.

Americans wanted to help. From states all across the country, people sent money for victims' families. Businesses donated food, water, ice, socks, and gloves for the rescue workers. Some people even sent special socks for the dogs so they wouldn't cut their paws on broken glass. New York City restaurants served free coffee and food to the rescuers, who worked 24 hours a day to find victims and clear the debris at "the pile," as Ground Zero was called for months.

At 8:30 P.M. on September 11, President Bush addressed the nation on television. He promised Americans

A New York City firefighter received a hug of encouragement from President Bush.

that emergency plans were in place to help the victims of the attacks. Praising the American people for their courage, Bush said:

> Today, our nation saw evil, the very worst
> of human nature. And we responded with
> the best of America—with the daring of our
> rescue workers, with the caring for strangers
> and neighbors who came to give blood
> and help in any way they could.

THE HUNT FOR AL-QAEDA

Only a few hours after the attacks, the Central Intelligence Agency (CIA) and the Federal Bureau of Investigation (FBI) began piecing together information about the terrorists. During the hijackings, flight attendants on all four planes had told headquarters the seat numbers assigned to each terrorist. The government soon had a list of 19 possible names and began investigating. It quickly became clear that al-Qaeda and Osama bin Laden were responsible for the attack.

President Bush ordered his advisers to find bin Laden. The CIA knew he was in Afghanistan but didn't know his exact location. The government of Afghanistan was run by a group of people who sided with bin Laden. This group, called the Taliban, agreed with al-Qaeda that American foreign policy was hurting Muslim culture. Although the Taliban was not responsible for the September 11 attacks, it did not want bin Laden brought to justice in the United States. Bush asked the Taliban to turn over bin Laden to the United States, but it continually refused.

The United States decided to send U.S. military troops into Afghanistan to capture bin Laden and other members of al-Qaeda. U.S. military battles in Afghanistan, called Operation Enduring Freedom, were aimed at pun-

U.S. military forces began arriving in Afghanistan in October 2001.

34

The 26th Marine Expeditionary Unit flew by helicopter to an undisclosed location on December 14, 2001, as part of Operation Enduring Freedom.

ishing al-Qaeda for attacking the United States and at removing the Taliban from power because it protected bin Laden. Although the United States was successful at finding some top al-Qaeda leaders, but bin Laden avoided capture.

35

In the months following the events of September 11, the people of the United States tried to get on with their daily routines. New York Mayor Rudolph Giuliani encouraged New Yorkers to return to work, go back to school, and go out to movies and restaurants. He refused to let the terrorists make Americans afraid.

Construction on the damaged Pentagon building began. Pentagon officials promised to repair the damage in one year. They completed the rebuilding in just nine months, on June 11, 2002. Workers placed a special brick in one of the new walls. Part of the debris, the brick was black from the fires

Mayor Rudolph Giuliani

that burned for 12 hours after the crash. Workers engraved "September 11, 2001" on it and placed it in the new wall.

The cleanup in New York City took many months. Crews removed 1.8 billion tons (1.6 billion metric tons)

A plaque with a quote by President Bush stood outside the Pentagon during reconstruction in March 2002.

of metal, concrete, office equipment, and other debris from Ground Zero. On May 30, 2002, the last steel beam was removed from the site. Firefighters, police officers, and families of victims lined each side of the path as the last workers passed by with the beam draped with an American flag. Many victims were never found, although rescue crews worked day and night for eight months to find every possible person.

Ideas were proposed for how to develop the land where the Twin Towers

The final steel beam, draped in black cloth and a U.S. flag, was removed from Ground Zero on May 30, 2002.

On March 11, 2002, twin beams of light pierced New York's night sky for 32 days in the spot where the Twin Towers once stood. They commemorated the six-month anniversary of September 11.

once stood. Many victims' families thought the site should be made into a September 11 memorial. The owners of the land wanted to put up new buildings and revive business. In January 2004, a memorial design was chosen from more than 5,000 entries. Because so many people were deeply affected by September 11, there were several debates over what, if anything, should be built on Ground Zero. More than 5,000 ideas poured in. The final design was meant to recognize both the importance of remembering September 11 and the need to move forward.

The attacks of September 11, 2001, changed most Americans in some way. Many became more fearful of the world. Others volunteered more often to help victims of disasters. Many men and women joined the military to defend the United States. Countless Americans shared deep gratitude for the brave first responders who tried to save as many lives as possible.

About 25,000 people were rescued or escaped from Ground Zero. Mayor Giuliani called it the greatest rescue in New York City history. One year after the tragedy, Giuliani reflected on the courage of the people of New York. He said, "The attack was intended to break our spirit. It has utterly failed. Our hearts are broken, but they continue to beat, and the spirit of our City has never been stronger."

The spirit of America was not broken on September 11, 2001. Rather, the American people worked together to repair the damage and mend shattered lives. The tragedy united

A 3-year-old girl held the American flag at a September 12, 2001, candlelight vigil. The flag became a symbol of hope for Americans in the aftermath of September 11.

Americans and showed their courage and strength in the face of the most deadly and frightening attack in modern American history.

GLOSSARY

command centers—temporary headquarters at a disaster site where orders are given

evacuate—to leave a dangerous place and go somewhere safer

first responders—professionals and volunteers who are the first to help in an attack or accident

Ground Zero—the site in New York City where the Twin Towers of the World Trade Center once stood

hijack—to take control of an airplane or other vehicle by force

Islam—religion founded on the Arabian Peninsula in the seventh century by the Prophet Mohammed

Muslims—people who follow the Islam religion

Pentagon—large office building in Arlington, Virginia, that is headquarters for the U.S. Department of Defense

rubble—broken bricks, concrete, glass, metal, and other debris left from a building that has fallen down or been demolished

terrorist—a person who uses violence to kill, injure, or make people and governments afraid

42

DID YOU KNOW?

- The two World Trade Center towers, each more than 1,350 feet (411 meters) high, were the tallest buildings in the world until 1973 when the Sears Tower was built in Chicago, Illinois. It took six years and eight months to build the towers and only 102 minutes to destroy them.

- In February 1993, terrorists exploded a truck bomb in the parking garage of the North Tower of the World Trade Center. Six people died, and about 1,000 were injured.

- The Pentagon, built during World War II, covers 29 acres (11.7 hectares) and has 17½ miles (28 km) of hallways. More than 23,000 people work there for the U.S. Department of Defense.

- It has been estimated that it cost the terrorists $400,000 to $500,000 to carry out the September 11 attacks.

- When the Federal Aviation Administration (FAA) grounded all flights on September 11, 2001, it was the only time in American history that all planes in the United States were ordered to land immediately. No commercial planes were allowed to take off for nearly two days.

IMPORTANT DATES

Timeline

SEPTEMBER 11, 2001

8:46 A.M.	Airplane hits the North Tower of the World Trade Center in New York City.
9:03 A.M.	Second airplane hits the South Tower of the World Trade Center.
9:05 A.M.	President Bush receives the report of the second crash.
9:25 A.M.	The Federal Aviation Administration orders all airplanes over the United States to land.
9:37 A.M.	Third airplane hits the Pentagon near Washington, D.C., killing everyone on the plane and 125 workers inside.
9:59 A.M.	The South Tower collapses.
10:03 A.M.	Flight 93 crashes in a field near Shanksville, Pennsylvania.
10:28 A.M.	The North Tower collapses.
8:30 P.M.	President Bush gives a televised speech to the nation.

IMPORTANT PEOPLE

MOHAMMED ATTA (1968–2001)

Member of al-Qaeda believed to have flown the first plane into the North Tower of the World Trade Center on September 11, 2001. Born on September 1, 1968, in Kafr El Sheikh, Egypt, Atta later graduated with a degree in architecture from Cairo University.

OSAMA BIN LADEN (1957–)

Founder of the terrorist group al-Qaeda and believed to have planned and paid for the September 11, 2001, attacks. He was born in Riyadh, Saudi Arabia, to a wealthy family with ties to Saudi royalty.

GEORGE W. BUSH (1946–)

President of the United States when the country was attacked on September 11, 2001. After the attacks, Bush and the U.S. Congress created the Department of Homeland Security to protect the United States from future terrorist attacks and to respond to natural disasters.

RUDOLPH GIULIANI (1944–)

Mayor of New York City from 1994 to 2001 including during the attacks on the World Trade Center. For his leadership in the aftermath of the attacks, he was named Time *magazine's Person of the Year for 2001.*

WANT TO KNOW MORE?

At the Library

Ganci, Chris. *Chief: The Life of Peter J. Ganci, a New York City Firefighter.* New York: Orchard Books, 2003.

Goodman, Robin F., and Andrea H. Fahnestock, eds. *The Day Our World Changed: Children's Art of 9/11.* New York: Harry N. Abrams, 2002.

Lalley, Patrick. *9.11.01: Terrorists Attack the U.S.* Austin, Texas: Raintree Steck-Vaughn, 2002.

Louis, Nancy. *Ground Zero.* Edina, Minn.: Abdo Publishing Company, 2002.

New York Times Company. *A Nation Challenged: A Visual History of 9/11 and Its Aftermath.* New York: Calloway Editions, 2002.

On the Web

For more information on *September 11,* use FactHound

to track down Web sites related to this book.

1. Go to *www.facthound.com*

2. Type in this book ID: 0756520290

3. Click on the *Fetch It* button.

Your trusty FactHound will fetch the best Web sites for you!

46

On the Road

Winter Garden at the World Financial Center

West Street between Vesey and
Liberty streets
New York, NY 10281
212/417-7000
A glass-covered indoor garden that
overlooks the Ground Zero site

The Pentagon

Pentagon Tour Office
Washington, DC 20301
703/695-3324
Headquarters of the U.S.
Department of Defense

Look for more We the People books about this era:

The 19th Amendment
ISBN 0-7565-1260-3

The Berlin Airlift
ISBN 0-7565-2024-X

The Dust Bowl
ISBN 0-7565-0837-1

Ellis Island
ISBN 0-7565-0302-7

The Great Depression
ISBN 0-7565-0152-0

The Korean War
ISBN 0-7565-2027-4

Navajo Code Talkers
ISBN 0-7565-0611-5

Pearl Harbor
ISBN 0-7565-0680-8

The Persian Gulf War
ISBN 0-7565-0612-3

The Sinking of the USS Indianapolis
ISBN 0-7565-2031-2

The Statue of Liberty
ISBN 0-7565-0100-8

The Titanic
ISBN 0-7565-0614-X

The Tuskegee Airmen
ISBN 0-7565-0683-2

The Vietnam Veterans Memorial
ISBN 0-7565-2032-0

A complete list of We the People titles is available on our Web site:
www.compasspointbooks.com

INDEX

About the Author

Mary Englar is a freelance writer and a teacher of English and creative writing. She has a master of fine arts degree in writing from Minnesota State University, Mankato, and has written more than 30 nonfiction books for children. She continues to read and write about the many different cultures of our world from her home in Minnesota.